Baby Massage

Parent-Child Bonding Through Touch

Amelia D. Auckett

Newmarket Press • New York

6 7 8 9 0 F/C

Photographs by Csaba Banki
Family photographed: Ken, Paola and Bianca Mellor
Line drawings by Rhyllis Plant
Design by Gene Siegel

Library of Congress Cataloging in Publication Data

Auckett, Amelia D.
  Baby massage.

  Bibliography: p.
  Includes index.
  1. Infants—Care and hygiene.   2. Massage for children.   3. Parent and child.   I. Title.
  RJ61.A86   649'.122   82-2172
  ISBN 1-55704-022-2   AACR2

QUANTITY PURCHASES
Companies, professional groups, clubs and other organizations may qualify for special terms when ordering quantities of this title. For information contact: Special Sales Dept., Newmarket Press, 18 East 48th Street, New York, New York 10017, or call (212) 832-3575.

Manufactured in the United States of America

Critical acclaim for Amelia D. Auckett's
Baby Massage—

"*Baby Massage* is timely since many western cultures finally appear ready to learn—and benefit from—infant massage. Auckett's volume not only delivers the message that early massage is nurturing, it also teaches the techniques to all those concerned with the care and nurturing of infants."

—Tiffany Field, Ph.D.
from her Introduction

"This book offers guidance and assurance for those who want to grow close to their babies through massage. (Plus it's fun and inexpensive.) The heart of the book is the technique chapter, which describes in detail how to stroke and touch each part of the baby's body."

—*Bookmarks* (Newsletter of the International
Childbirth Education Association)

"*Baby Massage* is the first book to explore not only the philosophy of baby massage, but its techniques. Utilizing an abundance of photos and diagrams, this guide can be used by interested new parents as well as more experienced individuals."

—*The Midwest Book Review*

Contents

5

List of Illustrations

Acknowledgments

There are many people who have contributed their energies and time to this book, so to all the loving friends who have helped, I wish to express my sincere thanks.

In particular the following have provided both tangible and intangible help which I gratefully acknowledge. They are mentioned in alphabetical order.

Dr. David Bannister for support, encouragement, manuscript readings and quotable correspondence; Penelope Goward for reading and commenting on the manuscript; Ralph Hadden for work with early drafts of some chapters; Ken Mellor for many readings, a large contribution in one chapter, help with editing, suggestions and general support; Barbara Robb for several readings and helpful creative suggestions; Rick Webb for help with typing, editing, ideas, index and support and nurturing; and many mothers and babies for their involvement.

I give special thanks to my teenage sons, Paul and John, for their cooperation and for their caring and interest in my book.

Preface

Baby Massage was first published in Australia in 1981, and in the United States in 1982. Since then, many hospitals in Australia and in other parts of the world are teaching parents to massage their premature babies. Some hospitals are also teaching parents to massage their full term babies, incorporating touch as part of the total care of the infant, along with bathing and feeding, believing it is of the utmost importance during a baby's earliest years. The teaching of baby massage also continues in our maternal and child health Centres.

My own interest in the subject began after I became aware of the baby massage work being done at the Mothers and Babies Health Association Hospital in Adelaide, Australia. There, in August 1977, I met and talked with Jacqui Showell, a physiotherapist at the hospital. Soon after my return from Adelaide, I introduced baby massage at my infant Welfare Centre, and now hold regular demonstrations and practice sessions for mothers as well as for infant welfare nurses and other child care professionals.

We continue to hold Family-Baby Massage Workshops on weekends. Each family includes parent/s and baby. After we talk about massage, I demonstrate the massage on one of the babies. The parents then massage their babies with supervision. We usually have six babies at these workshops. After this, the parents and professional people taking part in the workshops can each experience a head and shoulder massage. As one father said: "This has allowed me to understand what the baby experiences." It also teaches parents how to give and receive nurturing. Family massage incorporates a positive interaction of the whole family through a shared learning experience, resulting in improved communication, enjoyment, relaxation, awareness and honesty.

I believe that it is the love that I express through my hands during a massage that has the power to help the baby heal and grow, and now this has been reinforced by scientific evidence. I call this massage the Touch of Love. Of course, the physical touch of massage is most important, but without love it is just another "therapy," and not a true shared experience.

I am appalled by the ever-increasing violence demonstrated throughout the world today, especially violence to children. If parents loved and respected themselves they would not inflict touch that hurts on their children. So, rather than simply teaching parents how to massage their babies, I am also teaching parents how to love and respect themselves.

The ancient art of massage is enjoying a rebirth throughout the world, and it is my hope that this book will make available new ways for people to love and care for themselves and their families. I believe in the effectiveness of baby massage, and I want to share what *I* have learned with mothers, fathers and people who work professionally with infants and families. I hope, after reading this book, you will *want* to massage your baby, and that you *will* massage your baby and gain as much pleasure and satisfaction from practicing the art of massage as I have gained from writing about it.

Amelia Auckett

Introduction
by Tiffany Field, Ph.D.

In her important guide to *Baby Massage*, Amelia Auckett notes that "the ancient art of massage is enjoying a rebirth throughout the world." Although infant massage has for centuries been an integral part of parenting in several African, Indian, and South Pacific cultures, modern western civilization appears to have been waiting for some blessing from the scientific community before accepting this rewarding practice.

And we have such evidence at last. Studies done over the last two decades *do* seem to suggest that infant massage is not only safe and pleasurable for babies, it actually appears to enhance infants' physical growth and development, as well as their developing relationships with parents.

In a recent study on premature infants, for example, our team of doctors and psychologists were able to document these positive developmental effects: Twenty very premature infants were given 45 minutes of massage per day for 10 days before they were discharged from a neonatal intensive care unit. Those infants, as compared to a control group who did not receive massage, *averaged 47% greater weight gain during the massage study, were more active and alert, were more responsive to social stimulation, and were discharged 6 days earlier at a hospital savings of $3,000.* Eight months after this same study, the massaged infants were still showing greater weight gain and superior motor and mental development.

While massage may not be as crucial for the already normal growth and development of full-term babies, massage would certainly enhance their physical well-being and their growing relationships with their parents. This advantage is clearly illustrated in *Baby Massage*.

As Auckett suggests, the art of baby massage teaches parents how to give and receive nurturing. "The massage continues the bonding process and helps establish a warm, positive parent-child relationship." This message is the essence of *Baby Massage*. Auckett also presents the very practical value of massage for nutrition, for reducing stress, for alleviating colic, for growth and self-healing. The massage techniques she has found effective for the various regions of the body are thoroughly described and beautifully illustrated with parent-baby photographs that clearly show the enjoyment felt by both. Auckett even discusses the beneficial effects of massage for special needs infants, such as blind or deaf babies, adopted babies, hyper- and hyposensitive babies, and premature babies with specific problems such as difficult breast feeding, sudden weaning, teething, and constipation. Auckett concludes her volume with a fascinating description of the use of infant massage in various parts of the world including Nigeria, Uganda, India, Bali, Fiji, New Guinea, New Zealand, Venezuela and the Soviet Union. We in the West could learn a great deal from these examples.

Baby Massage is timely since many western cultures finally appear ready to learn—and benefit from—infant massage. Auckett's volume not only delivers the message that early massage is nurturing, but also teaches the techniques to all those concerned with the care and development of infants.

Tiffany Field, Ph.D., has been studying and writing about early child development for over 10 years, focusing especially on infants' first contact with their parents and the outside world. She is currently doing research on premature infants at the University of Miami Medical School. She is the author of numerous books on early child development.

1

Birth and Bonding

Experience this with me:

I'm a very little person.
I'm completely surrounded, supported, nourished,
    warmed, cushioned
Swimming in a warm sea
I am one with my mother
At one with my newness
Feeling, hearing a heart beating, blood
    rhythmically surging around me, feeling safe
    and warm.
There is movement, this way and that
I am one with my mother's feelings; I feel it too
    when she is angry, sad, loving, happy.
With my mother, I experience other people, hear
    their muted sounds, feel their touch.
I am very small, surrounded by a supporting,
    nourishing, vast, loving universe.

As I steadily grow
My limbs stretch and flex
Against the soft boundaries of my world
And my back is caressed.
Then gradually my space becomes crowded.
I curl up
I curl into a ball
I feel confined, cramped
I long to stretch
To be free!
Then, dawning joy,
Rhythmical pulsations press me
And caress my skin,
Becoming stronger
As I start moving down a narrow tunnel.
Strong emotions and sensations
Surge through me.
It's time to be born!
Time to leave the warm womb
Time to experience my new life
The strong pressure eases
As I emerge—
I am free!

Gentle hands lift me onto
My mother's smooth skin,
We lie belly to belly
I feel her warmth
I hear again the familiar rhythm
Of her heartbeat.
I open my mouth
I cry once, then again,
As air fills my lungs
Then I breathe strongly.
Nuzzling her breast

My face pressed to her,
I find the nipple
Warm food flows into my mouth as I suckle.

Then I feel her stroking my head
And body—my back, my limbs.
My cord is cut,
Ending links with the womb,
Yet I feel safe
With our new bond already strong.
Our energies merge in a flow of love
As we look at each other,
As I hear her voice
And I respond to her touch,
Her smell, her taste.

Here, close to mother
I feel safe, nourished, warm
I belong.
I am.

Inside the womb, the baby has a rich sensory input, the sounds of the mother's own body and sounds from the outside world, movement as the mother moves, and a high tactile input with the baby completely surrounded and supported all around by the womb. Every emotion the mother feels has its physiological effect on her body, and the baby, intimately connected to her, experiences these too.

During birth, the baby undergoes an immensely strong, almost overwhelming experience, squeezed by powerful uterine contractions and moved down the narrow birth canal and out into the world.

By being placed gently on the mother's bare belly before the cord is cut, he will feel at peace and secure as he has eye contact with his mother and is caressed by her, and nuzzles and finds her breast. It is interesting to note that the umbilical cord is generally just long enough so that the baby can suckle. at the breast. The stimulation from this suckling releases hormones—oxytocin, which stimulates lactation and contracts the mother's uterus, thus assisting in the expulsion of the placenta, and prolactin, the other hormone, which induces the production of breast milk.

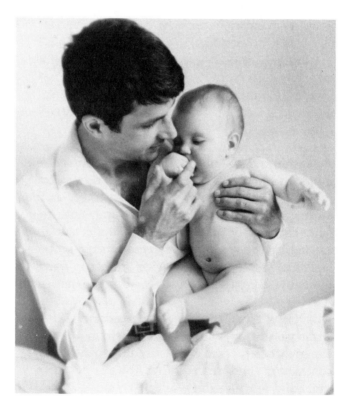

In the womb and during the process of birth, the umbilical cord supplies all the oxygen the baby receives, until the baby emerges into the air and takes his first few breaths. At this stage, oxygen comes from these two sources, the cord and the air, and dependence on the umbilical cord ceases only when the special valve in the baby's heart closes so that the pulmonary system takes over for the rest of his life. It is therefore important that the cord is cut only when it stops pulsating, so that the changes from womb to world, from depending on the mother to oxygenating his blood with his own lungs, becomes a smooth transition. This is a beautiful time for all, and is involved in allowing mother and baby the close contact they need while they are physically linked and are making the transition to another form of bond.

This is the moment for massage to begin. Very lightly. Very lovingly.

Since Frederick Leboyer's book *Birth Without Violence,* was published in 1974, many parents want to have a "Leboyer birth" for their baby.[1] This is a gentle birthing process that takes place in great silence with low lighting and gentle, loving hands allowing the baby to learn to breathe before the cutting of the cord; then allowing time for suckling at the breast—and for bonding—before he is given a warm, relaxing bath.

This kind of birth is available in some maternity hospitals around the world. However, more parents are deciding on home births of the Leboyer type, where there are minimum medical, technological and nursing procedures to interfere with the normal birth process. Thus the birth experience, the bonding and the welcoming time all belong to the parents and their new baby. The mother and her baby are not separated. They are close together, where they belong, and soon get to know each other, the father at their sides, involved, loving and bonding too.

Bonding is the strong physical, emotional and spiritual attachment which can develop between people of any age. Mothers, fathers and babies need a special time together immediately after birth for this attachment to develop. Bonding between parents and their new baby is a very significant event.

The importance of bonding through skin contact and close body contact straight after birth has been carefully described in the book *Maternal-Infant Bonding,* by M. H. Klaus and J. H. Kennell.[2] They have called this time "The Maternal Sensitive Period." I have heard Eva Reich call this period "The Welcoming Hour."

Bonding is developed by the baby through touch, sight, hearing, taste and smell. Behavior by the mother and father such as fondling, kissing, cuddling and prolonged gazing is an indicator of bonding attachment to their baby.

The ideal birth I have described is not always possible. Sometimes things go wrong and skilled medical help is needed.

Events which interfere with the bonding process are: delay in infant and mother and father being together after birth; drugs which anesthetize either the mother or the baby or prolonged separation after a caesarian section; the necessary use of the Isolette. Massage given to such babies by a person other than the parent can reduce

many of the harmful effects of separation. If,
when the mother or father is available, she or he
massages the baby, this, together with other forms
of closeness, such as cuddling, rocking and
holding, will reinforce and continue the bonding
process. The opportunity for bonding that would
otherwise have been lost can thereby be salvaged
and the bonds strengthened.

Often the procedure in hospitals during the so-called normal birth involves noise, bright lights, separation from the mother and little opportunity for bonding. In addition to these insults, the baby has undergone the turbulence of the birth itself, suffered the loss of security he had known in the warm womb, and the shock of finding himself in the isolation and emptiness of the bassinet. He is also denied the nurturing contact he needs. Massage is valuable for these babies too, as it is particularly effective in reducing the consequences of birth trauma.

2

Loving Touch

Massage is an expression of love through a special kind of caring touching. When mothers massage their babies at an early age, the massage continues the bonding process and helps establish a warm, positive parent-child relationship. It also creates a metaphysical energy flow, which could be called a flow of love between mother and baby. This is an energizing experience, and deep communication is possible. Baby massage is an introduction of caring touch that can continue to any age. Toddlers, teenagers and adults seem to be more receptive to touch if they were massaged as babies. Either parent can massage the baby. However, in what follows I am talking mainly about mothers.

Nutritional Value of Touch

Human touching provides a vital nutriment for the baby. All babies need a balanced diet, including the right vitamins and minerals, and if, for example, the premature baby does not have extra iron added to his feeding, he will develop anemia, with a consequent setback to his normal development. With an adequate supply of iron, such a baby follows a normal developmental pattern and thrives. So it is with loving touch. If there is a lack of this, the baby's emotional and physical development is impaired; if it is given freely, he develops normally, becoming healthy, vigorous and aware.

Massage for the Unsettled Baby

In discussion about baby massage with Dr. David Bannister, a Melbourne pediatrician, he had this to say:

Sometimes mothers and babies don't "click" or bond automatically, and if the baby is a difficult "colicky," irritable, nonresponsive baby, then the mother may have difficulty coping, adjusting or understanding her baby, and angry negative feelings can develop. The mother may draw away from her child, rather than toward him, and the interactions around this crying baby may sometimes engender hostile, aggressive feelings. The interjection of a positive, touching, caressing approach may be invaluable in altering the mother's negative reaction to a positive, tender, warm response. This can only be a good thing for mother and baby. I consider baby massage to be beneficial to baby from a very early age. It gives the mother something positive to do for her screaming "colicky" baby, and if it calms the baby down without the use of drugs, then this is a good thing. I think what you are doing in teaching the mothers to massage their babies is good.

Massage to Reduce Stress

Generally, baby massage is useful in reducing stress between parents and their babies. It is often very useful for mothers (or fathers) who were battered as babies and now find some difficulty in caring for their babies in a gentle, caring, loving

way. Through learning to massage, they find that
they can give their babies a pleasurable and
healing experience through touching. Moreover, a
mother (or father) who may be battering his or her
own baby is given an alternative, positive way of
interacting, a way that can soothe the baby's
crying and distress and enable both parent and
baby to feel happier in themselves and more
loving toward each other. I think that baby-
battering is often due to unresolved, excessive
stress, and I believe that the practice of baby
massage can do much to reduce its incidence.
Appropriate counseling, medical help or other
forms of support may also be needed.

Massage—An Alternative to Drugs

When through massage a warm, loving
relationship is developed, and a positive flow of
love is established between the parents and baby,
massage can become an alternative to drugs. The
love of the parent, directly expressed through
touch, promotes relaxation and encourages the
baby's growth and self-healing potential. Massage
is beneficial to babies in their developing years
and can remain valuable throughout their lives.
When early bonding is well established and the
mother-child relationship becomes warm and
caring, it lays the foundation for similar warmth
and caring with others in later life.

Parents' Experiences

I have seen satisfactory results with moderately
to severely unsettled babies and moderately to

severely anxious mothers. After massage the babies have become smiling and pink and very relaxed, and the mothers have become smiling and happy and have begun to enjoy their babies. The most frequent comment from mothers is, "It works, and I enjoy it too."

One mother told me how her baby always became excited and his eyes lit up when he realized he was about to have his daily massage, and I feel that this highlights the benefits of daily massage.

"Jane" started massaging her baby daily (full body massage) at six weeks of age. The mother appeared more relaxed after the massage commenced. She continued regular massage until the baby was eight months old. At this age, he was a responsive, active and very aware baby. Jane had commented when her baby was six months old: "It helped him to learn who I am and that I'm going to be there when he wakes up. I feel more aware of his body shape and the texture of his skin. I've gained a lot of confidence and I'm not scared to touch him; I just know we both like it." When the baby was eleven months old, she said: "I occasionally give him a full massage still, and recently when he was teething, I massaged his shoulders and neck. This was very effective in soothing him. I have not given any drugs to my baby in his eleven months of life."

I see this last statement as most significant. This baby, in fact, has not needed to get sick in order to have his needs met. This mother, with her loving caring touching and close communication, has met her baby's physical and emotional needs. Jane and her husband exchange massages, so that sharing pleasurable touching is a way of life in this family.

"Lois," who massaged her baby from six and a half weeks of age, commented when her baby was four months old: "I have touched something very delicate. It's beautiful. It's somewhere I haven't been before. I tune in as one—we become one." This mother was overanxious. Her baby cried a lot and had "colic." Merbentryl was given to the baby for four months. This mother had some full body massages from a professional masseur and some back and neck massage from her husband. Through being nurtured in this way, she was able to massage her baby to their mutual satisfaction and pleasure. It gave her something positive to do for her baby and calmed them both.

Lois goes on to say: "My baby is now nineteen months of age, and whenever I run my hands over his body, a pleasurable smile greets me; this, I feel, is a great gift which he has received for life, for he is now a responsive, lovable, affectionate human being in which massage would have played an important role."

I recently spoke to a group of mothers with toddlers of eighteen months, all of whom had massaged their babies. These toddlers showed a great deal of affection for their mothers and one another and played happily together. We held the group in the garden of one of the mothers. Instead of clinging to their mothers, these children played with toys, explored the garden and enjoyed themselves. They are very aware, responsive, stable children and have a lot of self-confidence.

These mothers still massage their toddlers from time to time, particularly in times of stress such as teething. One toddler, Nicholas, when he needs some attention, goes to his mother and pulls up his T-shirt indicating that he wants a "tummy tickle." Surely this infant has learned to get his needs met in a positive, enjoyable, open way. Each of three of these mothers is expecting a second child, and all three of them are going to massage their babies from birth onward.

In a questionnaire on baby massage one mother wrote:

> I feel it is important if you want to build a bond with your child. My son refers to his massage as "a tick a tick." He asks for it when he's upset; he knows it is something to make the "feeling" he has disappear. We have a very good communication level which I think is due to massage and body contact. When I started massaging him, we also developed a silent communication with our eyes. He is now able to tell whether or not I'm angry or pleased, through my eyes. I feel our relationship took on a new meaning when we started massaging at about two or three months. My son is nearly two years old now. The relationship is still growing.

Finally, another mother told me:

> I had no trouble in doing the massage, and I started when my baby was two weeks old. He is now twenty-five weeks old. I usually give him three or four full massages a week, then a massage of face and hands whenever I feel like it.

In the beginning, I massaged for ten minutes, and now take twenty to thirty minutes, unless he indicates that he wants a shorter time.

During the massage, my baby relaxes, smiles, plays with his own limbs, pats me and tries to talk. Afterward he is quiet and relaxed and sometimes sleepy. If we do a massage at about 7 P.M., he quite often sleeps longer through the night.

Apart from when he has wind, constipation or tummy aches, he usually cries only when he is hungry.

His ability to communicate has developed well, and he is bright and alert. I have quickly learned to recognize by his voice when something is wrong.

Massaging my baby has made me more confident with him; I am more relaxed and really enjoy this time together. After massaging the baby, I usually like to give my other son time and attention, and sometimes give him a massage too.

One thing I like is that the older children or their father can give massage to the baby. Communication is improved with massage, and I think it would be especially good for fathers, as they quite often spend so much time away from home. It is particularly good for fathers who have attended their child's birth, to keep the emotional bond going.

I have noticed that my baby is not only aware of his own body, but is more aware of other people.

My husband thinks massage helps to relax

the baby and to relieve any tension, and is good for toning up the baby's muscles after he has been lying down for any length of time. We prefer to use massage instead of medicines to calm him down after he has been upset. Many people have commented on how well behaved and happy our baby is on outings, and we assume they mean quiet and relaxed. We have always credited this to massage.

Benefits of Baby Massage

For mother or father:

Pleasure, enjoyment, permission to touch;
Communication, confidence, gentleness;
Relaxation, relief from anxiety;
Oneness with baby;
Something positive to do for baby;
Energy sharing between mother, father
and baby.

For baby:

Pleasure, joy;
Permission to touch and be touched (this
will flow on to later life);
Communication, closeness, gentleness;
Relaxation, calmness;
Reassurance through skin contact;
Better sleep pattern;
Development of body awareness;
Interruption of the anxiety–pain cycle,
improving digestion;

Improved circulation, increasing resistance
to illness;
Oneness with mother, father;
Emotional contact;
Energy sharing between baby and mother,
father.

Ashley Montagu in his important book
Touching[3] says that when certain young animals
experience skin stimulation, the immune system
benefits, resulting in a positive improvement in
disease resistance.

He believes it probable that human skin touch
can help in the growth of "healthy emotional or
affectional relationships."

He makes the important observation that being
loved, when learning to love, is superior to
instruction in loving.

Energy Exchange

Parents and professional people often ask, "But
what do you mean by energizing, exchange of
energy, and the needs of a baby to get subtle
energy from his mother?"

Some babies are jaundiced at birth or soon
after, because of a blood problem, and need an
exchange transfusion; that is, their blood is
gradually removed as they slowly receive
completely new blood *from another person.* This
allows the baby to survive and live a normal,
healthy life. This is a physical exchange.

However, an energy exchange cannot be seen,
but it can be felt, and the result can be seen, as
illustrated in the following example:

In the family massage workshops that I run with Terry Suckling, there is always a baby that is upset and crying and doesn't want to be massaged. We suggest to the mother that she have a head and shoulder massage, and within a few minutes of Terry starting the massage on her, the baby calms down, even though he is being held by another person—usually me. By the end of the massage, in about twenty minutes, the baby is in a deep sleep and usually sleeps for over an hour. This is a positive example of an energy exchange.

Energy exchange is very aptly explained by Jean Liedloff in her book *The Continuum Concept*[4] when describing her experience with the Yequana Indians in Venezuela:

> In the infant kept in constant contact with the body of a caretaker, his energy field becomes one with hers and excess energy can be discharged for both of them, by her activities alone. The infant can remain relaxed, free from accumulating tension, as his extra energy flows into hers.

In the Parenting Workshop which I attended in 1977, Ken Mellor, a Melbourne social worker, talked about ways of handling a frantic screaming baby who is not hungry or sick. He stated that, in his exerience, what these babies often needed was *subtle energy from their mothers.* If the mother was depleted, he suggested that she be nurtured in order to foster the flow between herself and her child.

I have held some of these frantic babies and

have felt them drawing energy from me.

However, if the baby's need is to discharge energy rather than receive it, going for a brisk walk or dancing around the room with baby in your arms or supported in a sling will often calm him down, as his energy flows into yours.

It is heartening to see that more parents are becoming aware of the benefits of body contact with their baby, because it promotes this energy exchange.

There is an energy link between the mother and baby which is involved in giving the baby his security. Without this link the baby is very likely to become distressed because he feels cut off from his mother.

This energy bonding is a most important part of mothering.

Parents who massage their babies, expressing their loving caring through touch, experience the flow of love energy. As this life energy is allowed to flow in babies and adults, it promotes self-healing, resulting in happier, healthier people.

Close Body Contact

There are other ways of continuing skin contact and close body contact in a loving way besides massage. The baby can have a bath with either of the parents. Fathers often enjoy a bath with their new baby. (Japanese parents and children bathe together until the children are about ten years old.) Breast feeding is also an important way that baby can experience skin and close body contact. Bottle feeding while the baby is against bared breast or chest is a variation on this. Some parents are finding that if their baby is unsettled at night, and they take baby into their bed, he settles down with the close body contact and all sleep well. This can be particularly effective if the baby decides to scream at 3 A.M.! Others extend this principle by having their baby sleep with them until some months after the birth.

In our society, babies often spend a great deal of time alone in bassinets, bouncinets, carriages and carry baskets. Carrying an infant in a baby sling gives the baby much needed body contact. The baby feels the rhythmical movement of his mother's body, hears her voice and heartbeat and identifies her unique body scent. He feels secure. This is a practical way of caring for the baby and doing housekeeping tasks at the same time, hanging out the washing or doing the shopping. A baby cannot be "spoiled" by close body contact.

3

Technique

Basically, the massage flows from top to toe, simply starting at the head and following on to face, neck, shoulders, arms, chest, belly, legs and feet. To finish the front of the body, use long, light strokes from neck to toe. Then, turning baby on to his belly, you massage his head, neck, back, buttocks, legs and feet. Again, finish with long sweeping strokes from head to toe. The whole massage takes about twenty minutes, or however long you and your baby want to take.

It is important for both adults and babies that all massage be given in a symmetrical way, that is, on both sides of the body, left and right. If only the left or the right side of the body is massaged, it can result in a feeling of imbalance, with one leg or one arm feeling "alive and lighter," and the other leg or arm feeling "heavier," leaving a sensation of being unfinished.

Kind of Touch for Your Baby?

begin with, use the lightest feather-touch, rease the pressure if you sense your baby's need for it. This is because many people (and babies are people) differ in their tolerance to degrees of touch. Your baby will let you know with joy the best touch to use.

Stroke or massage each area of the body described two or three times. On small areas use just the fingertips; for large areas use the fingers and palm. Some parts of the body will be massaged with one hand, other parts with both hands used simultaneously.

In the description to follow, "stroking" means just sliding lightly along the surface of the skin; "massaging" means gently moving muscles beneath the skin. Throughout the massage, you can change back and forth from the light flowing stroking to the slightly deeper, localized massaging, but always finish with light strokes so baby will stay relaxed.

Strokes should be flowing and free and need not be restricted exactly to the area described. When stroking the neck, for example, each stroke will naturally flow on to touch the shoulders and upper back, or when stroking down the arm, each stroke will include the fingertips and move beyond them.

It is best to have short fingernails when massaging anyone, but especially babies. If you must have long nails, make sure you use the balls of your fingers and the palms of your hands, and do not scratch baby. At the beginning of the massage, after washing your hands, rub them together until warm.

Is Oil Necessary?

When the light touch is used for baby massage, oil is usually not necessary. When massaging the back, oil can be useful, especially if the mother's hands have become moist. If you do use oil, I recommend a cold pressed vegetable oil (apricot or almond is suitable), obtainable from most health food stores. A cold pressed vegetable oil will nourish and moisten the skin, feels very smooth and pleasant, and it won't harm baby if he sucks his hand. The daily use of oil is particularly helpful if your baby has very dry skin. In the winter, warm the oil by placing the oil bottle in a container of hot water. Do not pour oil directly onto baby's skin, but pour a little oil on your own hand, hold it briefly to allow it to warm or cool to skin temperature, then smooth onto the part of the baby's body which you are about to massage. Do not use oil on the face; it is neither necessary nor pleasant.

Babies Under Four Weeks
(Including Premature Babies)

Give the baby only a short massage, approximately ten minutes.

Use light gentle strokes, being aware of sensitive areas. Many young babies at first don't like being touched on the head (particularly if the head experienced a lot of pressure during birth); also be gentle with the neck if at birth the cord was around the neck. You can accustom the baby to a gentle touch and soothe away the hurt gradually, with each massage, by increasing the length of time you stroke the sensitive area, from a few seconds to a minute or so.

Bath time is a good time to massage young babies, as it eliminates the need to undress and dress the baby an extra time.

Also, with young babies, massage can be done without completely undressing the baby; for example, the abdomen and legs can be exposed while leaving on upper clothes.

Do what the baby enjoys and respond to his needs.

The First Time

I suggest that the first time you massage your baby, you do it only when you and your baby are relaxed and happy and the baby is not hungry. If you do this, there will be imprinted on the baby's body memory association of the massage with a relaxed and happy feeling. After the initial association is made, you will later be able to use the massage to soothe and calm your baby when he is upset.

Should you start feeling upset while doing the massage, just go with the feeling; you are probably experiencing his pain (for example, his birth trauma) or getting in touch with pain you experienced early in life. If the baby becomes upset too, stop and give him a cuddle, as massage should be a pleasurable experience.

Work out a time that suits you both for your baby's daily massage.

Become familiar with as much of the technique as possible before you begin, by reading it through a few times.

Types of Massage

There are two types of massage. The first type is for pleasure and fun for both you and your baby; the second is for sharing, that is, a loving exchange of energies between you and your baby. This flow of love brings a special kind of closeness to you and your baby and allows the life energies to flow. It gives you both an increased feeling of well-being. Combine these two types of massage, and peacefulness, pleasure, fun and a wonderful communication between you and your baby will begin.

Massage Is Communication

A great deal of communication takes place through the eyes. So during the massage, be in eye-to-eye contact with baby as much as possible. Part of flowing communication involves flexibility, so be flexible. If the baby wants to turn around or change position somehow, don't forcibly hold him in position so that you can do that step of the sequence; just massage the part of the body that is accessible to you then, working in the head-to-toe direction. You can return later to the areas you missed.

You are probably aware that your baby, like an individual, is special and unique and has his own likes and dislikes, including where and how he likes to be touched. He is able to communicate this to you. So listen to, look at and feel what he is saying about his long-term dislikes or short-term dislikes; for example, "Today, I don't want my face touched." In this way, you can discover the strokes that you and your baby most enjoy and develop your own special style of massage, which will change according to your baby's needs and growth.

There are some babies who basically have a highly sensitive temperament or low threshold of sensitivity and cannot tolerate too much stimulation for too long. For these babies, begin by giving very gentle, short massages, gradually lengthening the time as their tolerance to loving touch increases. Occasionally a baby may not be responsive to massage, however, gentle. If this is so, try increasing close body contact and skin-to-skin contact in other ways. For example, the baby may be held against the bare chest of the father or mother. Remember that loving, caring touching is needed.

The massage can be poetic, sensual and fun; an art, not just a mechanical technique. As you massage, enjoy feeling the softness of his hair, appreciate the beautiful shape of his arm, talk to your baby, tell him what lovely eyes he has, tell him, "Your skin is just like velvet."

Preparation

Prepare the room beforehand, so that it will be warm for baby. Turn on the heater or open the drapes allowing the warm sunshine and light to stream into the room. Disconnect the telephone and close the door. Take off your jewelry, remove your shoes. With baby lengthways on your lap, head toward your feet, sit comfortably on a cushion on the floor, with your back supported, or in a bean bag, in the sunlight or in front of the heater or open fire with its golden glow of warmth. Alternatively, place baby on a yoga mat or sheepskin on the floor and kneel beside him.

Undress baby completely, but if he seems to be cold, cover parts not being massaged with a blanket. Place a towel under baby's bottom and have some diapers at hand, for the sign of a good massage is a good wee.

You are now ready to begin.

The Beginning

This is an important moment. A loving sharing is going to take place and this is something special between you and your baby. Be calm, be peaceful. Listen to, look for, and feel the body language of your baby. Ask yourself, "How does he feel right now?" Then talk to him. Tell him how you feel him to be as you start slowly and gently to stroke him.

How to Massage Your Baby

The Front of the Body

The Head

Stroke the crown of the head with one hand, using a circular movement. Be gentle with, but do not avoid, the fontanel, or "soft spot." Then, with the fingertips of *both* hands, stroke from the crown of the head down along the sides of the face.

The Face

With the fingertips, lightly stroke the forehead from the center to the temples, then lightly massage temples using a circular movement. Stroke the eyebrows from nose to temple; the bony ridges below the eyebrow and below the eye to the temple, from the nose, over cheeks to the ears. With fingertips, stroke from the corners of the eyes down the sides of the nose to the corners of the mouth; stroke from center of the chin along the jawbone to the ears. Stroke behind each ear starting at top. Stroke the ears back and front, following the shape of the ears.

The Neck

Very gently stroke the neck down from ears to shoulders and from chin to upper chest.

The Shoulders

Stroke from the neck to the beginning of the arms.

The Arms

Stroke down from the shoulder to the fingertips. Then wrap your fingers and thumb around the arm and do a series of gentle squeezes, starting at the top of the arm and finishing at the wrist. Use alternate hands. Massage the wrist using thumb and forefinger.

The Hands

Massage the hands, using the thumb for the palm, and the fingers for the back of the hand. Stroke each finger with the fingertips and thumb.

The Chest

Using both hands, stroke the chest from the center outward to the sides of body, toward the back. Remember that the ribs curve and strokes should follow the spaces between the ribs (the intercostal spaces). Stroke the diaphragm along the edge of the rib cage.

The Belly

Use a clockwise circular massage around the umbilicus, in ever-widening circles. Do this only after umbilical cord has separated (dropped off). This massage follows the course of the ascending, transverse and descending colon. Use the fingertips or the fingers and palms of hands.

The Genitals

Include in long strokes down the body, so that they are touched naturally as part of the whole body, not ignored, not accentuated.

The Legs

Massage thighs, knees, shins and calves. Then gently squeeze from thigh to ankle (as with the arms).

The Feet and Ankles

Massage the ankles, then in turn, supporting each ankle securely with one hand, use the thumb to massage the foot firmly from heel to toe along the sole of the foot. This is the firmest massage of the whole body. Stroke each toe, perhaps playing "This Little Piggie."

The Whole Front

Using both hands, one for each half of the body, stroke from neck to toes including the arms and genitals on the way. This long light full-body stroke can be repeated several times.

The Back of the Body

Turn baby over onto his belly and lay him across your thighs. Alternatively, if the baby is uncomfortable lying on his belly, hold him close to your body with his head just above your shoulder, so that his body is slightly curved. The back of the body can then be massaged, as he usually relaxes in this position. This is also a good position for the older baby having his first massage.

The Head

With the fingers and palm of hand, stroke the crown of the head down toward the neck until the bony ridge of the skull is reached (the occipital region).

The Neck

From the top of the neck, using both hands simultaneously and with one or two fingers, gently massage the muscles at the side of the cervical spine, using a descending circular motion, to the base of the neck.

The Shoulders

With the fingertips, gently move the muscles in a circular motion from the neck out toward the shoulders. Often your baby feels tense exactly where you feel tense, so if you are tense in the shoulders, give your baby some extra massage on his shoulders.

The Back

With your hand stretched out across baby's back so that your hand is in contact with the whole width of his back, stroke down his back from neck to buttocks, including the buttocks. Then, with the fingertips of both hands, lightly massage the muscles on either side of the spine, from neck to buttocks again, using a descending circular movement.

The Buttocks

Jiggle the buttocks around playfully.

The Legs

Give long strokes from the top of the thighs to the toes.

Full Body Strokes

From head to toe, starting on the crown of the head, with the fingers and the palm of the hand, give a long, light, loving, sweeping stroke down the back and finish beyond the toes. Repeat several times.

You have come to the end of the massage. Turn baby over, cover him with a blanket and hold him for a few minutes before dressing him.

Enjoy the moment!

As Your Baby Grows

The technique I have described is especially suitable for babies in the first nine months, but you can, of course, continue massaging your child effectively to any age. Toddlers, teenagers and adults can all benefit from massage. The same techniques can be used for older babies, though as they grow stronger you can massage more firmly. When introducing massage to older babies and children, choose a time when they are quiet, relaxed and receptive to stroking—perhaps at bath time or when they are sitting on your knee listening to a story.

Creative Touches

You can experiment and find many other ways to touch and play that will delight you and your baby. Try licking, for example. This could be particularly soothing on the eyelids (see Chapter 5). Kissing on the soles of the feet is another possibility. Tracing his body with your hair. Try Eskimo nose massage—use your imagination and your nose!

4

Massage for Babies with Special Needs

Massage can have a very beneficial effect on premature babies, emotionally disturbed infants, babies with physical handicaps and those experiencing a development lag. It can also help prevent early negative experiences such as separation from their mothers, and painful nursing or medical procedures from adversely affecting their behavior in later life.

Because of the calming effect of massage on mother and baby, as already noted, I think that it is particularly useful for the unsettled, irritable or "colicky" baby, making the use of sedating drugs unnecessary. Some of these drugs are obtainable without prescription and are often used by mothers.

Blind or Deaf Babies

These babies would become more aware of their body shape and of themselves as a person.

Sandra Weiss, in *Nursing Research* (March/April 1979),[5] says:

Jourard (1960) demonstrated that a person's perception of how much of the body is touched by others appears distinctly related to that person's positive evaluation of self.

The literature consistently shows that an individual who receives body contact from others over most body areas, in contrast to only a few areas, generally feels more attractive, feels closer to other persons, possesses an accurate perception of the form and shape of his body and has a positive liking for himself.

Elizabeth Panengyres (Physiotherapist-in-charge, Princess Margaret Hospital for Children, Perth, Western Australia) has observed a blind and deaf baby who loved a whole-body massage, and a postmeningitis baby, twenty-three months old and ambulant, who enjoyed modified massage.

She also knows an eighteen-month-old postmeningitis, visually handicapped, quadriplegic boy who enjoys a face and leg massage, and she will gradually try to increase the area massaged as his sensitivity decreases.

Babies in the Pavlik Harness and the Dennis Brown Bar

A number of babies with congenital dislocation of the hip have attended my Infant Welfare Centre. They had the Pavlik Harness applied a few days after birth. This harness is kept on all the time, except when a new harness is fitted.

No bath is given to the baby during the time
he is in the harness (six to nine months, followed
by the Dennis Brown Bar to approximately twelve
months). His face, limbs and bottom are washed,
but his trunk is mostly covered with the straps of
the harness, so skin stimulation in that area is
minimal.

I taught these mothers to massage their babies,
using apricot or almond oil and sliding their hands
underneath the straps of the harness where
possible. They reported that the babies really
enjoyed their daily massage.

I believe that the sensory stimulation which
these babies received during massage, which
otherwise they would not have experienced, has
been of tremendous benefit, and has made it easier
to adjust and catch up with their "milestones,"
such as pulling themselves up, when they are
finally taken out of the harness and bar.

Adopted Babies

Massage can be particularly useful in
establishing a bond between two strangers.
Adoptive parents literally become parents
overnight. As these parents miss out on feelings
stimulated by pregnancy and childbirth, massaging
their babies helps them to relate closely and gain
confidence in handling them.

In a recent massage practice session, I was
thrilled to see, when an adoptive mother first
started massaging her "new" ten-week-old baby,
the look of recognition and smile of acceptance
that passed between them as they established eye
contact and the mother began to explore her baby

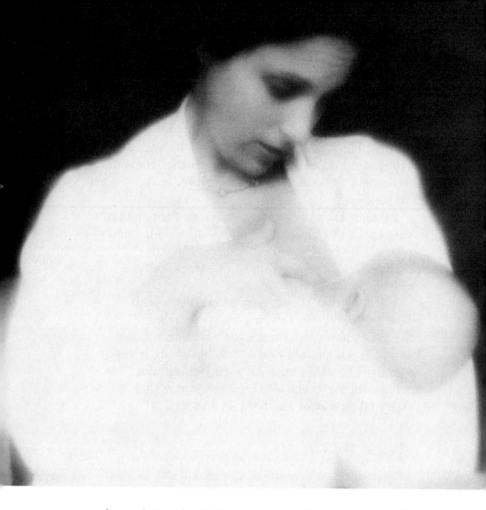

through touch. This was a special moment for all three of us.

The Hypersensitive Baby

Occasionally, babies do not like to be touched at all. One mother of such a baby had this to say: "Baby was extra sensitive. Nobody could nurse her but me, not even her father. She would panic if you took her anywhere there was a crowd. I

never let anyone nurse her, and I didn'i
out unless it was absolutely necessary.
daily massage helped her a lot. Now, a
months, there is no sign at all of her e
sensitivity. No drugs or medication of ...,
were used."

Massage was done on this baby daily—
gradually building up to about twenty minutes—
over a period of six months. The difference in this
baby when I saw her and handled her at nine
months was remarkable. She was smiling and
happy and certainly did not mind being touched.

The Limp, Lethargic Baby (Hyposensitive)

By contrast to hypersensitive babies, the
hyposensitive require much more stimulation
before they respond. Such babies can be
stimulated gently by massage, rather than relaxed
by it. Various forms of light tickling and a gentle
but firmer pressure may be useful as they are
massaged.

Premature Babies

These babies can gain great benefits from
massage, as described by Eva Reich in Chapter 5.

If baby has not been given massage in the
hospital, the mother can start when she gets home.
Often these babies need to learn that touch is
pleasurable, since much that they have
experienced at others' hands has hurt.

It is known that premature babies have
reasonably well developed nervous systems which

allow them to interact with their environment through touch, sight, sound, smell and taste, and that many of their interactions are not pleasant, but uncomfortable or painful because of procedures, monitoring, taking blood samples, etc.

Dr. David Bannister (see Chapter 2) says of one small hospital: "We certainly encourage gentle handling by the parents and sensory input through sound as well, by the parents making a tape of their voices and playing it inside the Isolette. I certainly would be keen for massage to become a regular part of the program for premature infants."

Massage is also becoming a regular practice with premature babies in some major maternity hospitals.

In such places, daily massage is given to unsettled, sensitive babies, or babies with a special problem.

It is valuable to help mothers who are apprehensive or nervous about their "fragile" babies. They can watch a trained person do it and then do it themselves with this person standing by to help and give advice.

It can be started several weeks before the baby is due to go home. During this period the mothers are shown how to massage their babies and are given practice sessions.

An interesting link has been established with Tim Adair, who read my article on baby massage in the *Australian Nurses' Journal*.[6] He is a pediatric physical therapist at the Research Medical Center in Kansas City. He is working on a research program of infant massage and stimulation with premature babies.

In October 1980 he was asked by the

neonatologist at the center to begin instructing several mothers from the Special Care Nursery in the Massage/Stimulation (Rice) method for these babies. (Dr. Ruth D. Rice researched and developed her Rice Infant Sensorimotor Stimulation [RISS] technique in 1975 [see Chapter 7]. This indicates a new approach in the United States to the care and development of the prematurely newborn baby.)

Some Specific Uses of Massage

Sudden Weaning or Difficult Weaning

A massage followed up by a bottle feed can be given in place of a breast feed if the baby is finding it hard to separate from his mother.

One mother, who had massaged her baby from a few months old, had difficulty in weaning her baby when he was nine months old. So at his usual time for a breast feed (this was the feed at which he was difficult) she massaged his back, feet, or wherever he wanted to be massaged. She then gave him a bottle feed, which he took without refusing it or becoming upset. The mother continued doing this for one month, and now her baby enjoys his 7 P.M. bottle and settles to sleep soon after taking it.

Difficulty Getting on the Breast

It is helpful to stimulate the rooting reflex in the new baby who has difficulty getting on the breast. The rooting reflex is part of the normal baby's in-built reflex patterning. The baby opens his mouth and makes jaw and tongue movements which indicate searching. Gentle stroking from cheek to mouth toward the chin stimulates the rooting reflex, and the baby increases his searching, nuzzling and the opening of his mouth in his search for the nipple, which can then be put in his mouth. The sucking and swallowing reflexes follow on, completing the entire feeding act.

Teething

If he has been massaged at an earlier age, massage can be very effective in calming the teething baby.

Stroke the top of the head and the forehead to the ears, including the temple. Stroke from the base of the ears down to the base of the neck. Then stroke from the center of the chin to the ears. Massaging the gums lightly can also be soothing. Mothers can use other body strokes that they know are soothing to baby.

Constipation

Abdominal massage can be very effective for babies with constipation. Use circular clockwise strokes around the umbilicus, thus following the course of the large bowel (see Chapter 3).

Getting to Know Me

During the massage, advance the baby's awareness of his own body by touching his hand or foot to other parts of his body. For example, rubbing his foot along the length of his other leg, so he develops a feeling of the size, shape, texture and special orientation of his body relative to other parts of him. Massage and self-exploration can be useful in preventing potential developmental and coordination problems.

5

Birth Trauma in the Newborn

In this chapter I have included contributions from other people. Dr. Eva Reich comments about gentle bioenergetic massage therapy of the newborn. Bioenergetic massage stimulates the integration and flow of body energy. Ken Mellor's contribution includes the way he handled the birth trauma of his daughter immediately after birth. Jacqui Showell gives a short summary of her work and involvement with the irritable, "colicky," supersensitive baby. (These "unsettled" babies often have a history of a difficult traumatic birth.)

Dr. Eva Reich, M.D.

The following ideas about bioenergetic therapy of the newborn have been expressed by Dr. Eva Reich in talks in Australia and other parts of the world. We have discussed these ideas together, and Dr. Reich has demonstrated these principles in workshops which I have attended.

Primal therapy of babies at primal times seems to be the answer to the problems of human beings who suffer from pain related to their birth and the neonatal period.

I developed a "butterfly touch" (a touch so light it does not remove the scales from a butterfly's wing) for the delicate massage of babies, in 1952, at the Harlem Hospital in New York City. It is based on the work of Wilhelm Reich, who first developed body therapy that he called bioenergetic medical orgone therapy. The technique is applied to the newborn for very brief periods of time, in a very lightly touching manner.

I think mothers, nurses and doctors, or anyone who has the care of newborn babies, could apply this massage technique if they understood the basic principle, which is that we work from the head toward the toes, very, very gently; that we try to flex the body into the attitude of orgasm reflex discovered by Dr. Wilhelm Reich, by bringing forward the pelvis and the shoulders; that we understand something about allowing the chest to really breathe out in expiration, and we learn to know where the tensions of the newborns are situated. When the baby responds, there must be something in the environment to return that response, otherwise baby has all reason to stay withdrawn.

Loving touch is important, and while doing the massage, tell the baby in a soft, gentle voice that he is welcome in the world, that you are sorry if he had a hard birth and that it is very good that he is now here and that everything will be all right.

Ideally, the massage can be done in the delivery room for babies, especially for those who have had a hard birth. (See pages 89–97 as to how two parents managed the difficulties of their baby immediately after a hard home birth.) Massage can also be done in special care nurseries where babies are undergoing various procedures.

Much body contact is the best natural therapy. The rocking motion of being in arms is excellent. A nonviolent natural birth and as little anesthetic as possible are also important.

Place the baby on his side to do the back, maintain eye contact, watch his facial expression, and work with the respirations of the anterior chest cage, aiding a wave of expiration to move toward the pelvis. This is a really good position, as the baby can be encouraged to flex.

The massage can easily be taught to the new mother. It is also important to work with the actual body tension and emotional reaction of the mother to the birth—her actual birth experience. I find the whole treatment works best when both the mother and the baby have a chance to express their emotions.

In talking about the small 1,500-gram premature infant, Eva Reich says:

It is important to stroke and stimulate and

massage and encourage the total expiration of the chest segment in the premature infant gently, because this will prevent the usual dependent pneumonias of the premature baby. In a series of babies that I did this with daily in Harlem Hospital in 1952, I found that none of them developed pneumonia, and neither did any of them die.

It is important to talk to the infant and tell him during the therapy that we understand that he is isolated, that he is having a difficult time in his infancy, that he is undergoing special procedures and that there will be a better time when he will go home to his mother. Treat him like a person who needs to understand what has happened to him.

It is very important that the person doing the massage loves the baby and that the touch be a loving touch.

I am convinced that the sleeping state—the withdrawal from the world of these premature infants—is an artifact of their environment, and in primal therapy people do reexperience the pain of their old isolation in the incubator.

I think all hospitals should welcome parents to be with their premature infants as much as possible, even if the infant is very tiny. (Incubators and "light treatment units" could be standing next to mother's bed, as in the maternity section of the General Public Hospital at Pithiviers, France, under Dr. Michel Odent.)

I also believe that mothers of sick neonates have the right to be there.

Hospitals need to treat little babies as people.

Ken Mellor

Ken Mellor is a social worker in private practice in Melbourne, Australia. He is experienced in child development and family problem solving, and is also experienced in Neo-Reichian therapy.

Ken, his wife, Paola, and their daughter, Bianca, are the people in the beautiful photographs in this book.

When I heard Ken talking about Bianca's birth at home, I wanted to include something about it in my book. Ken agreed to write out an account of the birth and the following few months of Bianca's life. It is such an interesting and important example of bonding, dealing with birth trauma and a father's involvement, love and commitment in caring for his baby, that I have included the whole account.

Imprinting

Right from the time we discovered that Paola was pregnant, I was determined to be present at the birth of our baby. I wanted to bond with her so that she would be emotionally linked to me as well as to Paola. When discussing this with a knowledgeable friend early in the pregnancy, he said, "You will probably not remember until the time, but do your best to have your upper body naked. That way, your baby will be able to smell your skin and feel what you are like much better than if you are dressed." This made a lot of sense to me, and I determined to do it. I already had plans of my own and added this to them.

When Bianca arrived, I was duly dressed so that my chest was ready for direct skin contact with her. I was wearing a dressing gown that was easy to open at the front. After Paola had held Bianca on her stomach and we had stroked her gently for quite some time and had put her to the breast, I took her. Before this, I had taken a fairly inactive role, as I did not want to interfere in the process taking place between them. However, at the point I took her, I wanted to be alone with her, and so be focused on her and she on me. So I stood up with her in my arms, held her out from me and looked at her. She opened her eyes and gave me a long searching look of recognition and acceptance. I pulled her into my chest and held her closely to me. Then, as I had planned previously, I licked her thoroughly on her forehead, her eyes and her cheeks. I had planned to lick her face completely, but when it came to the point, I found it too awkward to do this while holding her upright against my chest. Another time, I would probably put her on something soft and bend over her to do it. In this way, I could have reached all parts of her face and other parts of her body quite easily.

As I licked her, she seemed to relax; she seemed soothed. I was pleasantly surprised at the taste. In advance, I had imagined that it might be a little unpleasant. But I found this not to be true. If anything, the taste was neutral. My main discomfort through the process was that I thought others in the room may have been watching and I was a little self-conscious about it. I have repeated the licking on several occasions since and have received a consistently pleasurable response from her. She seems to find it comforting. I felt a connection with her at birth and have continued to do so.

All mammals lick their young with the tongue, except human beings, who touch gently with the fingers if not prevented from doing so. (See Ashley Montagu's book *Touching*.[7])

Dealing with Birth Trauma
Immediately After a Birth

Bianca's head was born and it was immediately obvious that she was in trouble. The cord was around her neck and had stopped pulsing. The doctor and midwife went into action: quickly they unwound the cord and pulled her out. Her neck was slightly twisted in the process. As soon as she hit the doctor's hands, she drew breath and started to cry. I breathed a sigh of relief.

This would have been enough trauma for any baby to have to deal with, but it was not all. Throughout the birth, Paola had been in considerable pain. Added to this, she had breathed through the pushing contractions and prolonged the second stage to about one and a half hours. The result was that Bianca's head was very molded. Some time after the birth, we noticed that there were three small bruises, almost abrasions, on the crown on her head. It was as though she had been scraped against something hard during the birth. This pressure was probably the cause of much of Paola's pain. In retrospect, it seems likely that she was in a transverse or posterior position and had sustained these injuries because of this. Meconium was on her crown when it was first visible, so she must have been in extreme distress from early in the labor.

From the moment of her birth, she whimpered and cried a little. She was not the peaceful, trauma-free baby we had wanted to deliver. Nor did she seem able to settle. We did all the necessary things: bonding, putting her to the breast, massaging her gently and the like. Also, because the doctor needed the information for his records, we did things like weighing her, and I kept hoping that she would settle down. But she did not. Instead, as time passed, she became more and more distressed. Even a warm bath did not help settle her.

After about two hours or so, she was crying in great distress. It was then that I noticed that the bruises on her head had become much worse. They had combined to form one large bruise which extended over about one-third of her head, a very blue, very painful-looking bruise. To relieve the pressure on this, we sat her upright in our arms and settled down to support her doing whatever she needed to do.

For about the next two and a half hours, she cried. She cried and cried, obviously in very great pain. Fortunately, we had many hours of sitting with grownups while they expressed the feelings—the pain—they had experienced during difficult births, and we knew two very important things. First, they had developed problems later as they had lacked support as babies while they expressed these feelings. Second, that the only way to express them seems to be to cry. So Paola and I simply held Bianca while she cried, occasionally taking turns when one of us needed a rest.

Quite quickly, it became apparent that she was working her way backward through labor. Her crying spells came in bursts, roughly timed at two minutes apart, just as Paola's contractions had been for most of the labor. Presumably each contraction had brought more pain to Bianca as the pressure on her head was intensified. At the end of each bout of crying, during which she was in acute distress, sometimes coughing and struggling for breath, she would either become very peaceful and look around at us, or she would sleep peacefully for a few minutes. Each time she quieted down, especially after she had been going for a long time, I hoped against hope that she was through it all and would stop. But she had not finished and would soon become distressed again.

I was very aware that it was my distress I was wanting to alleviate by getting her to stop, and that she needed to cry or she would not be crying. This made it only marginally easier not to interfere. Many parents would need a great deal of support to feel secure enough not to interfere. Thinking that something was wrong, which it obviously would be, and that they should do something besides feeling their own distress, they might try and jiggle or cuddle their babies to stop them. They might also succeed. But if they did, then they would also succeed in getting their babies to hold onto the pain of birth and to the subsequent limitations that would go automatically with doing so. They would also stop an apparent miracle, the miracle of the human being's capacity to heal itself.

As we held her, talked to her, told her we loved her and that we were sorry she was hurting, and that we wanted her to do what she needed to do, we watched this miracle take place. The bruising on her head went away, and so did the molding. After each crying bout, there was a little less of each. Eventually, there was virtually none left, and she rested peacefully for some time.

In the succeeding three or four weeks, she cried fairly regularly in a similar manner at first. It was obvious at these times that she still had more pain to release. Her cry when doing this was quite distinctive. However, the frequency dropped over this period, so that from being about once a day to begin with, it became about once a week. After two months, it was only once a fortnight, and now, at four and a half months, she seems to cry like this about once a month. Each crying spell has been from five minutes to one and a half hours.

The results have been worth it. There appear to be few if any residual effects of the birth. Also, Bianca impresses us and others as

being contented, alert, very relaxed and very responsive. Above all, she seems to be completely secure both with us and with our friends; not a baby who is scared of people who are apparently neglecting her because they sit with her and let her cry when she is in pain from the past. Finally, when she cries nowadays, we can tell what it is about. Almost always, it is about a here-and-now issue, and when on the rare occasions it is not, we can tell by the quality of her cry and know that the best thing to do is to hold her while she cries it out. I think that leaving her to do this alone, either earlier on or now, would have been, and still is, a very bad idea.

Jacqui Showell

Jacqui Showell is a physiotherapist, working in Adelaide, Australia, with the Mothers and Babies Health Association. She is particularly involved with the irritable "colicky" baby under four months, who she feels is often supersensitive to the environment and his own body. Jacqui says about her work:

I use massage in conjunction with handling techniques to give some continuation of the familiar uterine world. Included are handling the babe in flexion (similar to the usual fetal position), maximum body contact, slow, firm-cushioned movements, deep floaty baths, sheepskins to sleep on and being carried as much as possible in a sling on the parent's body. The parents may also attend my relaxation and discussion group and, where possible, receive some massage from me—for their relaxation, to get some nurturing and energy and to experience what they will give their babies.

The very young babies are always held in flexion, and they are massaged while they are in this flexed fetal position. Gradually they are helped to cope with more extended postures.

My techniques are adapted from my physiotherapy training. Gerda Boyesen's "bioenergy massage," as taught in her institute in London, and other forms of healing such as acupressure. However, most of my learning has been from babies and their mothers over a three-year period of intuitive exploration.

The flexed position, as illustrated on page 96, is a useful way to hold baby if he is upset and arching his back. The position of flexion relaxes his abdominal muscles, calms him down and gives you a free hand to answer the telephone, for example.

Another flexed position is with the baby curled up in the semifetal position on his side, his head forward on his chest and his knees drawn up to his belly. This is a good position in which to massage the premature baby.

6

Nurturing and Support for Parents

I have been emphasizing the baby's needs for loving touching, but in this chapter I turn to the equally important subject of meeting the needs of the parents. The emotions and behavior of the parents and that of the baby have a strong influence on each other, so it is vital that the parents, as well as the baby, have their needs adequately met.

The parents who are emotionally and physically well nourished are better able to provide the care needed for their baby's full development. They will also find it easier to cope with day-to-day management of the baby. Raw nerves and reliance on tranquilizers or stimulants can thus be lessened or eliminated.

Nurturing is being cared for, nourished, fed.

We all need nurturing, particularly at times when we have to give out a lot to others. Massage is an important and pleasurable way of receiving nurturing.

Some of the ways of being nurtured by others—partner, family or friends—are by having a foot, head or neck and shoulders massage, or a full body massage.

Think back to when you were a child. In what ways were you nurtured then? Think of things that made you feel good, such as sitting on your father's knee and being cuddled, having your hair washed or brushed or having your back scratched or rubbed. Do you ask your partner to nurture you in any of these or other ways now?

Self-nurturing

What is a self-nurturing experience for you? A bubble bath? An early night? An unhurried nourishing meal? Time to paint, enjoy music or read a book? Time to just be? Make time for some self-nourishment today—no matter how brief.

Support Systems

Because the "extended family" (more than two generations living together or nearby) seems to be diminishing in significance in our society today, it is important that parents with young children become aware of the supporting groups and services that are available, and learn how to use them. Examples include groups of nursing mothers and child-minding groups. Also, a circle of supporting friends, maybe including "foster grandparents," can be an enriching experience for parents, children and friends and can make the task of parenting easier to cope with.

Feelings

When a baby arrives in the family, particularly if it is a first child, many new and often unexpected stresses and tensions are added to the parents' lives, as changes in their relationships and routine occur. Previously buried feelings may surface in ways the parents find hard to explain.

At the time of the actual birth, the atmosphere of excitement, anticipation and, perhaps, fear, with the rhythmic contractions of the mother and then with the baby appearing, may cause many of those observing to be put in contact with their own internal feelings of being a baby and being born. These sensations can be very strong, and occasionally a person witnessing a birth may start to experience being confined and short of breath, to feel anger at the way the medical staff are treating the baby or to feel fear of any pain being experienced. But they may not be aware of why they are experiencing such strong feelings. (This may explain why some hospital staff are sometimes very anxious to administer drugs to the mother as she goes into strong labor—feeling panic and distress arising as they start to contact the memory of their own painful birth.) An attempt by someone to suppress any manifestation of birth feelings in someone else is probably an attempt to suppress it in themselves.

Parents also often have feelings of great joy and elation following childbirth, and sometimes experience a release of spiritual energy imme-diately after, and for several weeks after, the birth of their baby. This is a happy, important time in the lives of parents, grandparents, siblings and friends.

Flow with the energy of the feelings you have, so that the energy is supporting instead of conflicting; laugh if you are happy, cuddle if you are loving, cry if you are sad, go to another room and shout if you are angry or scared. Physically expressing strong feelings provides a safe outlet, thus avoiding a buildup of tension in our bodies.

Changes and Adjustments

With the addition of a baby to their lives, parents find that there are changes in their relationship and adjustments to be made.

The husband and wife change from being a carefree couple, usually with two pay checks and often living a full life with many outside interests, to parents with the constant responsibility of caring for their baby and less money to live on. Adjusting as parents is often difficult, although to some couples it comes naturally. In any case, with patience, understanding, love and sharing, successful adjustment can be achieved.

Your relationship as a couple is important, so make time to spend with each other at home. Share your life. Get a babysitter occasionally to mind baby (grandparents usually enjoy this job) and have a night out together.

For the mother, it often means being no longer in the workforce. This can involve loss of friends, loss of identity, loss of structure and loss of financial independence, resulting in feelings of grief. This loss of identity stems from being a capable, efficient and important person in her occupation and then, after the arrival of the baby, becoming a mother and being referred to as a "housewife" with little or no status. This often has a devastating effect on a woman, especially if she previously had an interesting career. She is sometimes lonely and isolated, relying on her husband to meet most of her emotional needs, and may develop the "suburban neurosis syndrome."

Also, a mother who has been brought up in a nuclear family often has no experience of handling small babies, and as a result is often anxious and scared about specific things and may be generally confused and lacking confidence. Nurturing from her partner, family and friends will help this mother to deal with her scared feelings; support and information as she learns to use it will help her with her confusion and lack of confidence. To be held, cuddled or caressed when feeling scared is comforting and reassuring.

Adjusting to the Baby

It takes time to get to know your baby. Take the time to do this. You may need to learn to accept being a parent and the changes it brings. Knowing that this takes time may help you to be at peace with yourself. This can be an exciting and rewarding time of your life. Being available to your baby will help you discover parenting as an on-going living experience. Enjoy as much of it as you can and practice being a creative parent.

Dr. David Bannister has this to say:

One of the things I find that is very important is the changes or adjustments parents have to make, especially with their first baby.

They can be told and warned, but it still comes as a shock to a lot of parents, particularly the first few weeks with a new creature they know nothing or very little about. I tell them that having babies is a lottery—you do not know what temperamental characteristics they have inherited from the parents, or what are their own entirely different ones. It takes time, sometimes, to get to know this new person, and it can be a very stressful time for *all*. It can also be fun and absorbing getting to know your own baby, but parents need to be given "permission" to experiment, to find out their baby's likes and dislikes and not necessarily stick to rigid schedules.

Where we, as health professionals, all too often go wrong, is in giving directions to parents, rather than advice or suggestions that might or might not work. We should be encouraging the parents to find out for themselves, i.e., develop their *own* parenting skills, rather than become dependent on others for what to do.

Stress

Hans Selye, in his book *Stress Without Distress*, says:

"Stress is the non-specific response of the body to any demands made on it—when we say someone is under stress, we usually mean excessive stress or distress."[8]

Stress can be produced from a pleasant or unpleasant experience. How we react to stress or distress is what counts. At childbirth and for about six to eight weeks after, mothers and fathers can be under excessive stress, especially if the baby cries more often than usual and both parents do not get enough sleep. One important way of dealing with stress is to find the cause and make some changes.

Mothers' Special Needs

If the mother is feeling exhausted and tired, perhaps it could be arranged for a relative or friend to help with the housework.

If the situation warrants, it might be arranged for someone to sit up with the new mother during the night feed for moral support, or for the husband or grandparent to give the baby the night feed for a few nights so that the mother can have a longer sleep.

If the baby is breast fed, maybe enough milk can be expressed during the day for a night feed. Lactation sometimes fails if the mother becomes too exhausted through lack of sleep. Having a sleep during the day or going back to bed after the early morning feeding are also ways of getting more rest and helping to maintain the milk supply.

In addition to being tired through lack of sleep, for the first few weeks after childbirth, mothers are often physically and emotionally depleted. What they are likely to need is caressing and energizing through loving touch. As sexual intercourse is generally not resumed until after bleeding has stopped, this closeness and body contact is often missing. Of course, couples can learn ways of sexually pleasuring each other without genital contact.

Massage can be a nonsexual nurturing and energizing experience for a new mother, renewing her energy level and so enabling her to meet the baby's need for emotional and physical nourishment. A back and shoulder massage can be given to the mother while she is sitting comfortably in a bean bag, perhaps while nursing or feeding the baby or maybe watching TV, and her husband can sit behind her to give the massage. More generally, mothers could ask husbands, partners, family or friends for some massage, or a hug, or a caress when they are tired or when they feel like being nurtured.

I believe that a full body massage given to mothers on the second or third day after childbirth and frequently during the next six weeks could help prevent postnatal depression, as mothers themselves often feel the need to be held and caressed during this time.

Physical Benefits for Mothers from Massage

Massage dilates the blood vessels, improving the circulation and relieving congestion throughout the body.

Massage relaxes muscle spasms and relieves tension.

Massage increases the blood supply and nutrition to muscles without adding to their load of toxic lactic acid. (Lactic acid is a by-product of muscular activity, produced when insufficient oxygen is present in the muscular tissue to prevent its formation. It is present in tired or sore muscles.) Massage thus helps to prevent the buildup of harmful "fatigue" products resulting from strenuous exercise or injury.

Massage helps you to feel good.

In Malaysia, mothers are massaged on their second or third day after the birth of their baby, and then every day for six weeks. The massage is usually done by the mother, mother-in-law, or even the grandmother. Australian women I have spoken to about this Malaysian custom respond with "Wow! Wouldn't that be wonderful."

Ashley Montagu, in his book *Touching*,[9] quotes Reva Rubin as saying that meaningful touch administered during labor, actual birth and immediately after birth influences the mother toward a more effective use of her hands, whereas remote, impersonal contact induces similar attitudes toward contact with her baby. Montague suggests that it may be a good idea for the husband to caress his wife's body "during pregnancy, labor and after the birth of the baby."

In some Melbourne hospitals, abdominal massage is given to mothers after childbirth by the physiotherapist. Why not back or indeed a full body massage?

It seems to me that home deliveries provide very well for the nurturing needs of mothers and fathers. As well as the doctor and midwife, there can be one or two support people, usually close friends or relatives, and the mother can receive a lot of physical contact and strokes from her husband and the support people, both during labor and after the baby has been born. Jealousy in siblings is generally unknown when they are part of the birth experience.

General Support

After the birth of a baby, whether at home or in the hospital, support, nurturing and help for baby, mother and father and other children are most important. Family and friends usually supply this support. However, where young families are isolated from their parents, people working with young families professionally can give very valuable support.

In the first few weeks after the baby is born, it is important that the new mother gets out of the house with the baby and has a break from the "at home" feeding, bathing, diaper-washing routine.

In my experience, these young mothers have a great need to talk about what is happening with them and their babies, and it often helps to know that other mothers have problems and feelings similar to their own. After six weeks, when the groups that I conduct finish, these mothers often continue meeting in their own homes as well as meeting again at the Health Centre with me at three monthly intervals. Firm supporting friendships are made, and as the babies become older, play groups are formed.

Many new parents, especially mothers, resist asking for help, believing that they should be able to cope with their baby and home, that if in fact they cannot manage by themselves, they are failures as mothers. But the real fact is that it is difficult for a mother to do all the caring for a baby and herself without help from her husband, family or friends. If isolation affects the mother in a negative way, this feeling is transferred to the baby. Babies benefit from extra contact with others, rather than just the mother and father.

I suggest that you ask for and accept help, and share your baby with others. It is all right to be helped!

Fathers' Special Needs

The family with a young baby can be seen as an energy circuit. There is the young baby needing energy, but the mother at this stage is often low in energy due to fatigue and the constant demands of her newborn baby. The father, who is stimulated by his activities outside the family, can be seen as a battery supplying energy to the mother and through her to the baby. The baby at this stage still belongs in the mother's energy field; that is, he still has a close energy link with his mother. The mother is the most important person in the baby's life. Fathers may experience themselves providing energy for everyone for some time—and they need replenishing, too.

This does not mean that fathers only have contact with their baby through the mother. In fact, it is important that they have direct contact with baby from birth onward and so build up a warm loving relationship with their child. Besides cuddling and holding the baby, father can feed the baby if bottle fed, bathe the baby or have a bath with baby—and massage the baby. Fathers who have been present at the birth of their child usually become more involved in the care of their baby, feel part of the whole birth experience and feel closer to their child.

If a father has paternity leave or a week off work when his wife comes home with the new baby, this gives him an opportunity to get to know the new baby and give practical support and help to his wife. If there is a toddler in the family, the father could spend a lot ot time with him, thus helping to eliminate some of the jealous feelings the toddler may have toward the new baby, and the mother can then give less divided attention to the new baby.

The father is a very important member of the family, but with the mother's time being mostly taken up with the care of the new baby, leaving little time or energy to share with her husband, he may feel neglected. Furthermore, the temporary cessation of sexual intercourse with his wife could result in him feeling the lack of intimate, pleasurable touching and caressing. However, this need not be the case if this couple had learned to relate nonsexually through close body contact and pleasurable touching without always having sexual intercourse or genital contact. This subject is sensitively explored in Helen Kaplan's book *The New Sex Therapy*.[10] A sensitive sensuous massage is one way of experiencing this.

I have talked to fathers about their needs and suggested that they have a weekly body massage from a caring person. While they agree that this is a good idea, they think it would be difficult to find such a masseur, the gym-type football masseur or the massage parlor masseuse being quite unsuitable. However, there are some caring masseurs, and maybe they could advertise as such.

I have been emphasizing problems, but I recognize that the new baby also brings with him or her many joys and satisfactions, and that parents, besides coping with the distresses, can have fun with their baby and experience pleasure and pride in nurturing their child.

A *conscious* awareness of your own needs and the needs of others makes it possible for the whole family to cooperate in getting their needs met in a positive way.

7

Baby Massage in Other Cultures

In this chapter I want to show that different cultures recognize the value of baby massage and close body contact; for example, by mothers using baby massage as a natural custom in the daily care of their infants and by constantly carrying babies close to their bodies. It is, however, not intended as a complete worldwide review of these practices.

Modern Western civilization is only recently rediscovering these practices and finding scientific reasons for accepting them. It is sad that in our Western society some of us have to learn *how* to touch and *be* touched lovingly. It is not this way in many cultures. For example, skin and body contact form an important part of parenting in many parts of Nigeria, Uganda, India, Bali, Venezuela, Fiji and New Guinea.

Many women in tribal, nomadic, urban or rural environments carry on their usual work with their babies contentedly supported in slings. Clothing is often adapted into slings for this purpose. These babies, close to their mothers' bodies, experience a rocking, rhythmical movement which can stimulate their motor and intellectual development.

Nigeria

Conversation with Aisha Abubaker, a mother and midwifery nurse educator from Nigeria, 1980:

Babies are massaged from birth until they are twelve months old, and it is usual for most mothers to massage their babies. This is a very old custom which is passed on from mother to daughter, and has now become part of their child care routine. Commonly, the baby is bathed twice a day, at 7 A.M. and 5 P.M., and then massaged with olive oil. Firm strokes are used. During the massage, the mother's hands are warmed several times by the charcoal fire or a heater.

After six weeks, the baby is likely to be massaged in a sitting position, helping to strengthen his back muscles in readiness to sit up alone.

Most mothers have their baby at home, or, if they enter a hospital, tend to stay for only six hours. Midwives practice in the community and also deliver babies in hospitals unless there are complications.

Baby is carried on the mother's back, secured with the mother's skirt—a long length of material which doubles as a baby sling and a skirt. A small towel or baby shawl is sometimes tied around the waist and under the baby's buttocks for added security.

For six weeks after childbirth, the practice is for the mother just to care for herself and the new baby. Other women in the family, usually the baby's grandmother, take over the work normally done by the mother. The new mother generally stays in her mother's house if they live nearby, and the husband visits her briefly each day. He is not very involved, as having babies is "women's business."

Uganda

Joseph Chilton Pearce, in *Magical Child*,[11] writes about the research of Marcelle Gerber, who in 1956 traveled to Africa to study the effects of malnutrition on infant and child intelligence. He says that Gerber, in Uganda, discovered that the Ugandan children were the most intelligent and advanced she had observed anywhere. It is significant that the children were delivered at home, usually by the mother herself; or if she was on the move, out in the bush. Separation, mother from child, did not occur. The mother massaged, caressed, fondled and sang to her baby constantly from birth. Carried in a sling, the baby was next to her bare breast and fed according to its own needs. The baby and mother slept together. These Ugandan babies were alert, happy and calm, and were awake longer than is usual. Bonding with their mothers was strong, with the mothers anticipating their babies' needs before they needed to cry for attention. For the first four years of life, Gerber noticed a superior intellectual development.

India

Frederick Leboyer, in his beautiful book *Loving Hands,*[12] shows the traditional art of Indian massage, which originated in South India and is passed down from mother to daughter. Throughout most of India, babies are regularly massaged from the age of about one month to six months. In the winter, diluted mustard oil is used, and in the summer, coconut oil. Leboyer says: "It is a sacred art in the true sense, since it is concerned with babies, with the renewal of life."

Bali

Speaking to a Balinese mother, I learned that in Bali babies are handled and stroked to comfort them. A child born in Bali is believed to have just emerged into this life from a spiritual realm and is regarded as holy. For about six months he is not permitted to touch the impure earth and is carried about by his mother or by older children, either in their arms or on their hips.

The Indonesian mother carries her child in a length of cloth known as a *kain panjang,* wrapped around her body. The child is carried in front for ready access to breast milk. As the child grows larger, he is carried on the side of the woman's body, still within reach of his food. Only after weaning is the child placed on the mother's back.

There is a strong folk tradition of massage in Bali. "Every single person" can do some massage, as many tourists have discovered.

If a baby in Bali has a pain in the gut, the

spirit doctor is called in. He massages the baby's belly with a mixture of coconut oil, a crushed, small red onion and salt. The massage lasts for about fifteen minutes. The baby is usually not fed for several hours, or until after he has used his bowels.

Fiji

Most Fijan mothers massage their babies with coconut oil following their daily bath. Massage is often given at night to settle the baby and to ensure that he sleeps well. Babies are carried close to the body in a sling fashioned from the mother's skirt.

New Guinea

In Wewak, New Guinea, the baby is carried in a "bilum" string carrier, with the handle as a band around the forehead of the mother, the baby resting on the mother's bare back. *Pikinini i cri long skin belong mama* is a common pidgin English remark heard when a baby cries, meaning "The baby is crying to be close to his mother's skin"; literally, "skin to skin." For feasts and special occasions babies, from one month of age, are rubbed or "greased" with coconut oil.

New Zealand: The Maori

Christine Macdonald, in her *Medicines of the Maori*,[13] says:

On the east coast the baby was covered with Muka scraping, the silky floss from the inner leaf of the flax. This they called *kukukuku*.

In olden times, this was the covering for the first two or three weeks of life. Morning and evening, this was removed, the baby washed, and then gently massaged, the mother using a little warm oil (usually from the titoki). The baby was again covered tightly in fresh warm leaves, the moss and cape. . . .

Massage was considered highly important and was continued for several years, the mothers using different movements of their hands. Knees and ankles received special attention, so that these joints would always be supple.

Massage the legs of your daughter,
So she will walk with grace
Across the plains (*maraes*) of
Poverty Bay.

Dr. T. Wirepa[14]

Maori women today have much body contact with their babies and frequently stroke them.

Venezuela

In her excellent book *The Continuum Concept*,[15] Jean Liedloff describes her experiences with the Yequana Indians in Venezuela.

She discovered that these people make use of the principle of energy exchange (see Chapter 2) between infant and caretaker when the infant is kept in close contact with the body of the caretaker. With close body contact, the baby's body energies are kept in a state of balance. The result is a happier, healthier child.

The Soviet Union

The following report is by Ross G. Mitchell:

Soviet scientists believe that exercises and massages promote the formation of new communications within the central nervous system and the development of greater motor potentialities in consequence.

Whatever the theoretical basis for massage, [many] mothers and doctors in the Soviet Union are convinced that it makes the body and limbs more supple, strengthens and tones the muscles and skin, and generally increases the infants' well-being.

In the Soviet Union, it is an accepted and . . . practiced part of child care. These mothers are taught to massage and exercise their infants from the first few days of life, and prominence is given to illustrations and descriptions of the technique in books and films on mothercraft. In residential homes for children much staff time is devoted to massage. Pediatricians and other health workers are sure of its value and counter the question: "Why do you do it?" with "Why don't you?"

Although massaging healthy babies is a custom virtually unknown in Western countries, except in immigrant communities, it is common in some parts of Africa and Asia.

. . . Can a technique practiced by millions of mothers be so unimportant?[16]

The United States

In the United States in 1975 the Rice Infant Sensorimotor Stimulation technique was developed and researched by Dr. Ruth D. Rice.[17] This consisted of stroking, massaging and rocking and is being accepted as a "new" technique to enhance the care and development of premature babies.

It was found that in the babies who received "The Loving Touch," as her technique is now called, there was a significantly greater neurological development, greater weight gain and a higher score in mental functioning than the babies receiving routine care.

See Chapter 5 for Dr. Eva Reich's work at the Harlem Hospital, New York, in 1952.

Massage is an expression of love through loving, caring touch.

Notes

1. Frederick Leboyer, *Birth Without Violence* (New York: Knopf, 1975).
2. Marshall H. Klaus and John H. Kennell, *Maternal-Infant Bonding* (St. Louis: C. V. Mosby, 1976).
3. Ashley Montagu, *Touching*, 2nd ed. (New York: Harper & Row, 1978).
4. Jean Liedloff, *The Continuum Concept* (New York: Warner, 1975).
5. Sandra Weiss, "The Language of Touch," in *Nursing Research*, March/April 1979.
6. A. D. Auckett, S.R.N., "Baby Massage: An Alternative to Drugs," in *The Australian Nurses' Journal* (Melbourne), November 1979.
7. Montagu, *op. cit.*
8. Hans Selye, *Stress Without Distress* (New York: Lippincott, 1974).
9. Montagu, *op. cit.*
10. Helen Singer Kaplan, M.D., *The New Sex*

Therapy (New York: Times Books, 1974).

11. Joseph Chilton Pearce, *Magical Child* (New York: Dutton, 1977).

12. Frederick Leboyer, *Loving Hands* (New York: Knopf, 1976).

13. Christine Macdonald, *Medicines of the Maori* (Auckland, N.Z.: William Collins, 1973).

14. T. Wirepa, from a proverb in an article on the genealogical origin of his wife, in *Te Toa Takati Magazine* (New Zealand) 1925–26.

15. Liedloff, *op. cit.*

16. Ross G. Mitchell, "Is Kneading Needed?" in *Developmental Medical Child Neurology*, 18 (1976), 1–2.

17. Ruth D. Rice, Ph.D., "The Rice Infant Sensorimotor Stimulation," in *The National Foundation, March of Dimes*, 1979. Newborn Behavioral Organization, Nursing Research and Implications (Allan Liss, Publisher, 1980).

Bibliography

KAPLAN, HELEN SINGER, M.D. *The New Sex Therapy.*
New York: Times Books, 1974.

KLAUS, MARSHALL H. and KENNELL, JOHN H. *Maternal-
Infant Bonding.* St. Louis: C. V. Mosby, 1976.

LEBOYER, FREDERICK. *Birth Without Violence.* New
York: Knopf, 1975.

————. *Loving Hands.* New York: Knopf, 1976.

LIEDLOFF, JEAN. *The Continuum Concept.* New York:
Warner, 1975.

MACDONALD, CHRISTINE. *Medicines of the Maori.*
Auckland, N.Z.: William Collins, 1973.

MONTAGUE, ASHLEY. *Touching.* 2nd ed. New York:
Harper & Row, 1978.

PEARCE, JOSEPH CHILTON. *Magical Child.* New York:
Dutton, 1977.

SELYE, HANS. *Stress Without Distress.* New York:
Lippincott, 1974.

Index

Ask for these titles at your local bookstore or use this coupon and enclose a check or money order payable to: **Newmarket Press**, 18 E. 48th St., NY, NY 10017.

Baby Massage
____ $11.95 pb (1-55704-022-2)
How to Help Your Child
Overcome Your Divorce
____ $14.95 pb (1-55704-329-9)
How Do We Tell the Children?
____ $18.95 hc (1-55704-189-X)
____ $11.95 pb 1-55704-181-4)
Inner Beauty, Inner Light:
Yoga for Pregnant Women
____ $18.95 pb (1-55704-315-9)
In Time and With Love
____ $21.95 hc (0-937858-95-1)
____ $15.95 pb (0-937858-96-X)
Loving Hands: Traditional Baby Massage
____ $15.95 pb (1-55704-314-0)
Mothering the New Mother, Rev. Ed.
____ $16.95 pb (1-55704-317-5)
My Body, My Self for Boys
____ $11.95 pb (1-55704-230-6)
My Body, My Self for Girls
____ $11.95 pb (1-55704-150-4)
My Feelings, My Self
____ $11.95 pb (1-55704-157-1)
Raising Your Jewish/Christian Child
____ $12.95 pb (1-55704-059-1)
The Ready-to-Read,
Ready-to-Count Handbook
____ $11.95 pb (1-55704-093-1)

Saying No Is Not Enough, Rev. Ed.
____ $23.95 hc (1-55704-324-8)
____ $14.95 pb (1-55704-318-3)
The Totally Awesome Business Book
for Kids (and Their Parents)
____ $10.95 pb (1-55704-226-8)
The Totally Awesome Money Book
for Kids (and Their Parents)
____ $18.95 hc (1-55704-183-0)
____ $10.95 pb (1-55704-176-8)
The What's Happening to My Body?
Book for Boys
____ $18.95 hc (1-55704-002-8)
____ $11.95 pb (0-937858-99-4)
The What's Happening to My Body?
Book for Girls
____ $18.95 hc (1-55704-001-X)
____ $11.95 pb (0-937858-98-6)
Your Child at Play: Birth to One Year, Rev.
____ $24.95 hc (1-55704-334-5)
____ $15.95 pb 1-55704-330-2)
Your Child at Play: One to Two Years, Rev.
____ $24.95 hc (1-55704-335-3)
____ $15.95 pb 1-55704-331-0)
Your Child at Play: Two to Three Years, Rev.
____ $24.95 hc (1-55704-336-15)
____ $15.95 pb 1-55704-332-9)
Your Child at Play: Three to Five Years, Rev.
____ $24.95 hc (1-55704-337-X)
____ $15.95 pb 1-55704-333-7)

For postage and handling, please add $3.00 for the first book, plus $1.00 for each additional book. Prices and availability are subject to change.

I enclose a check or money order payable to **Newmarket Press** in the amount of _____

Name_____

Address_____

City/State/Zip_____

For discounts on orders of five or more copies, contact Newmarket Press, Special Sales Department, 18 East 48th Street, NY, NY 10017; Tel.: 212-832-3575 or 800-669-3903; Fax: 212-832-3629.